TEACHERS ROCK JOURNAL

THIS JOURNAL BELONGS TO: